Table of Contents

As far as Internet marketing is concerned, Fiverr is a place both for beginners as well as experienced people. I always tell beginners to start their endeavors at Fiverr and use the money they make there to invest into building their business, or build it on Fiverr itself. I've convinced a bunch of my friends to do so and taught them to be successful. They now thank me for it and have happily provided their own experience, so I can share it with you.

Fiverr represents a whole world of opportunities to earn or get things done for you. It's a large website, well known and has a lot of visitors each day. Instead of building something from scratch, a beginner can leverage fiverr.com right away and literally start making money by tomorrow or even a few hours after creating the first gig. With the money earned by completing orders, you can get webhosting, domains, an auto responder and tools without having to invest into these things out of your own pocket. In addition, you get something even more valuable – experience from doing something, motivation and the feeling of accomplishment. Making that first dollar online is the sweetest moment, one you are unlikely to ever forget. Most beginners are confused and wonder what they could do, without ever making a dime online. With this guide, you're on the inside, so I urge you to take it seriously and take action! Making money on Fiverr has proven to be easy, if you take action.

How Much Earning Potential Is There?

When you first look at the front page of fiverr.com, your impression might be like my own:

1. Oh, such chaos … so many different gigs! So much competition!

2. Do I have original enough ideas to be a seller here? Do I need to be talented?

3. With only $5 per order, it seems unlikely one can make a lot of money here.

The first two of these are easily dispelled. It appears chaotic and there are many, many, many gigs, but the search function on the site and the sorting options make it easy to navigate them. People **will** find your gigs if you create them properly. Competition is no problem either, as long as you do your job well and aren't lazy. And talent? You don't need to be able to sing or play a guitar – trust me, there are things you can do. Remember the postcard gig I told you about? Or the one about writing a message in the sand? Even if you are the most untalented person in the universe, there are things you can do. In section 2 of this guide, I'll bombard you with ideas and explain how to implement them.

What about the third of these points? How much potential is there to make money?

First of all, the usage of Fiverr is completely free. When someone places an order, you get $4 upon completion, while Fiverr takes a $1 fee. It's the customer who pays the fee, not you. That's unless you order someone's gig yourself, thereby becoming a customer. Whatever you do, don't be deceived by the $4 and think there is no potential to earn.

But then, how much money is there to be made?

I'm happily going to prove to you now that it's possible to make $40,000 in as little as 6 to 8 months just by selling services on Fiverr directly. Please go to fiverr.com and search for, let's say, "backlinks" – or **click here** to get there right away. Now, at the top of the list, there are several options to sort it.

Click on "High Rating" to get the best rated gigs on top, and then click on the first gig. Since I don't wish to endorse a certain gig, I shall only show you the stats of what I find. Perhaps now that you are doing this yourself, you find a different gig on top.

On the right side of the gig page, you should see something like this (this screenshot is from the old design of the website). Now look, this seller has gotten 4649 reviews for this gig alone and has currently 368 orders in queue. Man, that's a lot of orders to work through! Many people don't review, or they review only once but order a gig several times in a row. I estimate this gig to have been ordered at least 6000 times. If you take into account that one order equals $4, you end up with $24,000. However, this seller offers an addition to his gig, which can be ordered as well, and that addition costs $10.

Fiverr takes 20%, or $2 of the $10, for itself. If we say that only 10% of all people who ordered this gig also got the addition, then the seller got another 600*$8 = $4800 in profits. If you also take into account the 368 orders still in the queue, you get another $1768, including the %10 who get the addition. Therefore, the overall profits of this gig are $30,568. From just 1 gig!

Next, click on the username of the person selling it to get to their profile page. Look at the top of the page to see how long the user has been registered. I'm now looking at someone who's been here for 7 months. This user has a few other gigs running – they are listed in his profile. From what I calculate and estimate, he has made over $50,000 in those 7 months since joining Fiverr.

Internet marketing gigs such as backlinking services are very hot and sell like warm bread (more on the Advanced Gig section). It's an evergreen terrain, because all webmasters need backlinks and will order them again and again. But no matter where you look, you'll find the same kind of success. If you click on any category on the right and sort by popularity or rating, each of the top gigs is one that has sold a great number of times.

Now listen, I'm not saying you are going to make that much money, nor am I saying you can make a lot of money quickly. All I'm showing you in this chapter is what's possible, and this is our motivation as we dive into the Fiverr Master Class. Even if you only make $500 in 2 months, it's still a lot of money if you happen to be a beginner, and you can use this money elsewhere to make more. Most beginners struggle for a long time, often years, before they make a dollar. But you are better off than most of them, for you have our master guide on a platform that makes it easy. Let's do it!

Important: Abiding by the Rules and selling Premium Services

It's very important for you to remember that sharing your email address or Skype username via messages on fiverr.com is against their Terms of Service (TOS) and can get you into trouble. You need to understand that it would otherwise be very easy for sellers to offer their services directly via PayPal, thus costing Fiverr the $1 fee they take for every order.

Never tell your customers directly to go to another place to purchase from you there. It's not fair to the people behind Fiverr, who have given us a great platform, and above all *it's not right*. When it's about money, people can easily be tempted to go down the wrong path, and I urge you not to allow yourself to go down such a path. Always do things right – anything else is just a headache. Besides, there are huge benefits to use Fiverr over saving that single dollar, as you will see in the next chapter.

Another reason to play by the rules is that PayPal charges a fee for getting payments. So if you got individual payments from customers, you'd lose some of the money you saved on the Fiverr fee, which means you don't even save the whole Dollar. If however, you withdraw the money you make on Fiverr in larger batches, you will pay a smaller fee on PayPal compared to the individual fees.

What you *can* do is attach your email address or Skype name in your message-attachments for quality assurance. This way you can make it a part of your customer care, which is a nice thing to have. You can also link to your website from your profile. Personally, I don't do any of this, but a few of my friends have done it successfully.

If you are more advanced in selling services on the Internet, you might have something to offer that goes far beyond an ordinary Fiverr gig. Maybe you design and maintain websites, or you are a programmer, or perhaps you do professional SEO. Whatever service it may be, it's likely more expensive and might even include a recurring payment. Let's say you have a customer on Fiverr who you think might be interested in your premium service(s). How do you get in touch with them?

In order to market a premium service to a customer who I thought might be interested, I used to link to a page on my website, essentially telling my customer that I offer "premium services that go beyond ordinary Fiverr gigs". In my experience and the experience of many others I have talked to, this is certainly acceptable, because it's something you aren't selling on Fiverr anyway.

My premium service didn't have its own website, so the page I linked to was plain white and pretty much said the same thing as my message, but it had my email address on it and asked to contact me for further discussion. In other words, my customer went to the page I linked, saw that I have a premium offer and sent me an email to discuss it. By using this method, I made almost more money from my premium services than I made on Fiverr itself. So as you can see, Fiverr is a stepping stone to (more) success in your other endeavors and thus far more powerful than most people ever realize.

To make absolutely sure you abide by the rules, I highly advise you to read the Fiverr Terms of Service, which you can find **here**.

The 6 Pillars of a Successful Fiverr Gig

When it comes to creating a successful Fiverr gig, we need a certain amount of creativity, a good idea, and a method behind that idea to make it happen. These are important factors for our product or service, but they are qualities existing *behind* the gig we are placing on the Fiverr website. A gig serves as the skeleton or framework of our service and is essentially a classified ad – the thing everybody sees and hopefully responds to. There are six main ingredients that make the difference between a successful and an unsuccessful gig.

1. The Pillar of Initiation

The title and picture we choose for our gig combine to the first impression a potential customer gets of it. Most dead and boring gigs I see display titles such as "I will design a logo for your website for $5" or "I will sing a custom birthday song for $5". Such a title is unlikely to cause people to react – we need to get our gig noticed in the blink of an eye! You can easily achieve that by adding adjectives, such as: "professional", "awesome", "creative", "killer", "amazing" or "excellent". In addition, you should also mention a strong benefit right after the adjective.

By including adjectives and writing them in capitals, our title stands out from the crowd and might very well get someone pumped to order our service over others. We can now enhance the boring examples by saying: "I will design a PROFESSIONAL, high-quality logo for your website for $5", or perhaps "I will design a KILLER original logo for your website for $5". And for the other gig, we could say: "I will sing a CREATIVE custom birthday song for $5".

Many people do the capitalization nowadays. It works, but there is a better way, and I really want you to get this. Do **not** write the adjectives in capitals! Instead, capitalize the words that describe your gig, such as "article" or "logo". A search engine gives higher importance to a fully capitalized word. We want the Fiverr search function to value "article" high, not "professional". People are then more likely to find your gig over your competitor's gig.

In addition to this, we can add phrases like "in 24 hours" or "free revisions" to increase the perceived value of our offer. If someone perceives our offer as valuable, they're more likely to place an order. Always make sure your title contains a keyword, which is a word or phrase that describes what your gig is about, so that people can actually find it when using the search function. Be descriptive in your title, but don't write too much; if it's too long, people are unlikely to read it. To get a better sense of that, I suggest you go to Fiverr and search for something, then observe which titles you actually read and which you just skim over.

Apart from a creative, eye-catching title, we need a custom picture for our gig that describes what it's about. The simplest thing you can do is to go to Google images and search for relevant pictures. Try not to take a picture from the very top, because they are widely used and might not look all that original. Scroll down a bit and see if you find something interesting you can either take or modify, perhaps by using parts of a second or third picture and putting them together to create a new one. But remember, you aren't the copyright holder of those pictures. Most people won't think or care about that, but if you wish to respect copyright, you can go to stock websites such as **www.sxc.hu** to get stock pictures for free and use them. Some of the pictures they have require that you tell the copyright holder you're using their picture. Luckily, most pictures can be used just like that. Always check the restrictions below "Availability".

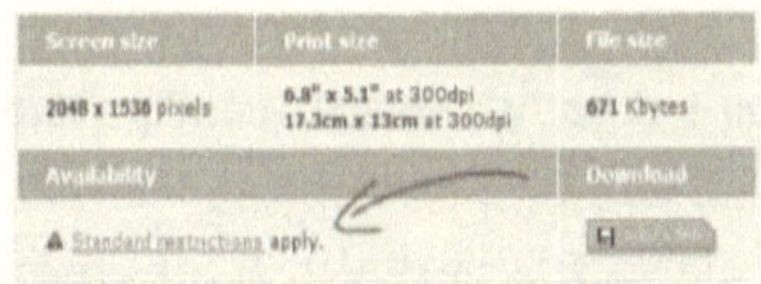

Screen size	Print size	File size
2048 x 1536 pixels	6.8" x 5.1" at 300dpi 17.3cm x 13cm at 300dpi	671 Kbytes
Availability		Download
⚠ Standard restrictions apply.		

Psychologists have shown that the first seconds of meeting someone can very well determine whether or not you like a person. People do judge a book by its cover, and they do it quickly. So whatever you end up doing, make sure you have a good-looking custom picture. My friends and I have found that a gig with a better picture and better title can increase its sales by up to 55%.

2. The Pillar of Motion

Fiverr gives you the option to upload a small video to your gig, which will be shown at the position where your main picture would otherwise appear. This is the single most important detail you can add to your gig and you always, always have to do this! You can simply combine a number of slides of text or pictures, while you explain what your gig is about. The main thing about your video is to mention fiverr.com – such as the phrase "only on fiverr.com" at the end of your video. You see, every video is manually reviewed and approved by a moderator, and if you use the name "Fiverr" several times, it is very likely for your gig to get featured. A featured gig appears alongside a few others at the very top on the main page and has the attention of everybody. I'm sure you see how powerful this is!

You can use software like **Animoto** (see Video 2) or **muvee Reveal** to create beautifully animated videos without any effort. Make sure you speak into your microphone, be charismatic and possibly entertaining, and try to be natural. Under no circumstance should you write plain text. Of course, you can also film yourself if you have a good camera – a face builds trust and sells better than random pictures.

If your gig is about singing a song, voice acting, filming yourself doing something funny, or anything like that, you absolutely need to use the video to present what you do to your potential customers. The same is true if you create animations, such as intros for videos. Make sure you use the video as an example, but remember to talk as well so you can mention fiverr.com.

3. The Pillar of Decoration

Since you will be using a video, you won't actually have a main picture. However, you can display up to four pictures, or three pictures and one video on every gig you create. Make use of the space you have, for it will make your gig look much more alive and inviting to potential customers. If you do anything artistic, use these pictures as examples of the results your customers can expect!

4. The Pillar of Detail

The fourth pillar of a successful Fiverr gig is the description, which is obviously the main part of it. You need to be clear, informative and professional about what you are offering. Make sure your grammar is good, too. Try to appear unbiased, experienced and authoritative to create a sense of hope that a certain problem will be solved by your service. If the nature of your gig allows it, you can also create a sense of urgency and instill the fear that your potential customers will be worse off if they choose to forego your service. All of these points are elements of effective sales copy.

The best thing in the world you can do in your description is to link to certain pages on your own website. If you don't have a website, it's advisable to get one and really make yourself shine. You can just go to blogger or WordPress.com and open up a free blog. Create a page for frequently asked questions (FAQ), one with the video on it where you explain in detail what you're doing, what's involved and why this is valuable, and a page where you explain the reason for negative reviews. Once you are a more advanced seller and have gotten many reviews, there are bound to be some negative ones. Even if you always deliver your work and everything is done well, a few people won't be pleased, anyway. If you have a page where you explain the reasons for those negative reviews and link to it in your description, people can check out your response to reevaluate you as a seller. This way you can take the power out of those negative reviews! I'll tell you what you can do to avoid negative reviews at the end of the introduction.

Like on Twitter, there is only limited space for your description, so linking to external pages like these allows you to go beyond this boundary and be more professional than other people. In addition to this, mention how many sales your gig already has. If you have 500 reviews but had 1200 orders, you need to show that in your description. People tend to go with a group or the collective decision of a group, so mentioning the amount of orders your gig has received can very well convince people to order from you. Should you have many years of experience in what you do, mention that as well to complete your masterful description. Optionally, you can also put a call to action at the end, such as: "It's only $5, so get yours/it now!"

5. The Pillar of Trust

It's important that your customers warm up to you a little bit and trust you. In order to achieve that, you need to appear human to them. Don't be too authoritative and cold in the way you write. Instead, always be polite and say "thank you" and apologize for mistakes or if your work is going to be slightly late. Your customers will understand and be prone to leave a positive review regardless. Even better, if they are happy and feel they know you a little bit, they are likely to return.

6. The Pillar of Growth

In the beginning, things might be running slow. Perhaps you get only one or two orders a day, but if you continue and get more and more positive reviews, you will rise in rank.

After completing 10 orders with excellent ratings and track record, you automatically get promoted to level 1. At this level, you get access to features that enable you to offer additional services for a higher price and thus generate a higher income. What's more, people will see your level 1 badge and immediately feel safer with you than with a seller who doesn't have such a badge on their profile and gigs.

After 50 orders within the past two months, while maintaining excellent ratings and track record, you get promoted to level 2. This level unlocks additional features, allowing you to increase your sales and get priority support. You also get a new badge, hence providing an additional feeling of security for everybody who sees it.

If you continue to sell in large volumes, maintain an excellent rating, have exceptional customer care and show community leadership, you can be chosen to become a top-rated seller. Top-rated sellers are chosen manually by the staff. You get a golden badge, additional features and radiate authority and professionalism to everybody who sees you. When I first became a level 1 seller, I suddenly got $60 worth of orders in one day. And remember, this was pretty much at the beginning of my time at Fiverr, since you only need 10 successful orders to reach the first level! Something like this also happened to all of my friends when they hit levels 1 and 2.

As you can see, the more you do the more you are going to grow. In time, you are going to get more and more recurring customers who put your gig into their favorites. On top of that, your mountain of positive reviews and badge are both going to convince a growing number of people to order from you – and these people will mention you to their friends, in forums, or on social platforms like Facebook and Twitter.

In the section about playing by the rules I urged you **not** to try and contact your customers outside of Fiverr and getting them to buy from you directly. Saving the $1 fee sounds good on first sight, but it's foolish. You see, with every completed order, people will give you a positive review (not all people do it, as some are lazy). Every order you complete gets you one step closer to the top-seller level, and every positive review will attract more customers. By selling outside of Fiverr, you are not only playing with fire, but also missing out on the Pillar of Growth. Few people realize that using Fiverr creates the momentum for more and more success.

A Bag of General Advice

1. Reviews are an Asset

The positive reviews you get on your gigs are an asset of your business and need to be treated that way. Always do what you can to deliver your work on time, and make sure it's worthwhile, because each negative review impacts the overall rating of your gig as well as your personal rating. Imagine what it would look like if your gig had a rating of 50% and as many thumbs down as thumbs up. I don't think it would ever come this far, because people would stop ordering your gig way sooner than that. But don't think you can just delete the gig and recreate it with a clean record. Don't think you can be lazy, because your overall rating as a seller will stay – and with a bad rating, you won't get to higher levels. Always do things right!

Go the extra mile and try to over deliver, which means doing more than you agreed to do. And try not only to deliver on time, but rather deliver early! For example, if your gig is about writing an article of 500 words, try to write 600 and deliver it a day earlier than agreed.

If you do that, people will be very pleased, leave a great review and are likely to buy again.
In addition they might give you a tip for your work, but more about that later!

2. Gigs en Masse

Creating gigs is free and Fiverr allows you to have up to 20 of them, so don't be conservative. I see a lot of people who have only one or two different gigs, with little or no sales. If you have 20 different gigs instead, more people will find your gigs and therefore find you. Even if each of them only gets one order in two days, that's still 10 orders or $40 per day. So don't hold back, any skill you have can be made into a gig, recombined and sold!

3. Beginner Startup

In the very beginning things might be hard. You won't have a single review,

so people won't know if you are worth the money. It might take a while –
perhaps one or two days, maybe a week for the first order to come. If your
gig is interesting and well presented, the first order should come fairly soon.
Make sure you do all you can to satisfy your customer, because the first
review means everything. When you deliver your work, politely ask a
customer to leave a review. It would be unfortunate if that first sale didn't get
you a review at all, hence leaving you in the "beginner condition".

If possible, ask a friend or family member to order a gig from you. This way
you can get a positive review very fast and if that person can profit from your
gig, then that's even better. A lot of people create a second account and order
a gig themselves, but Fiverr frowns upon such behavior, as it's not allowed to
have more than one account.

4. Name of the Game

If the gigs you are selling are within a specific field such as Internet
marketing or, let's say, SEO in particular, make sure you choose a username
that reflects this. This way you'll appear very targeted for the needs of the
people who are looking for this kind of service. If you appear as someone
who specializes in one area and has a name to go along with it, you are bound
to look more professional. People are more likely to feel they found exactly
what they were looking for. And as a more general advice, make sure your
username isn't strange, having lots of useless symbols or letter combinations.
Choose a name that sounds good and normal, like "MillenniumArtist", or
"SEOwizard". Avoid usernames such as "Xxbutterfly19xX" for obvious
reasons – I'm sure you're aware of how unprofessional this looks.

Account and Profile Setup

Before we start building a brilliant 

Fiverr business and start making lots
of money, we need to set up an account. Even if you have already done that, I
urge you to read this step, as I will also be talking about how to set up your
profile properly.

First go to **fiverr.com** and look at the top of the page, where it says "Join".

Click on it and you get redirected to a short sign-up form, which is self-explanatory – just put in your username, email address and password. Don't forget to agree to the terms of service and do the little calculation at the bottom right. Then click on the join button.

After joining, Fiverr sends you an email with an activation link to the address you specified. Go to your email account, wait for the email to arrive, open it and click the activation link to complete the signup process. Congratulations, you're now a member of Fiverr!

Next, let's set up your profile. Go back to fiverr.com and click on your username at the top of the page.

Setting up a good, unique looking profile is very important for success on Fiverr. You will find the best results if you use a professional, good-looking photo of yourself. We humans want to look at faces; we trust faces. Nothing sells as well as a kind and honest looking person. If you don't want to use a picture of yourself or don't have one, you can use a stock photo from **http://www.sxc.hu**, the stock website I already mentioned once before. It doesn't really matter if a photo of you or anybody else, since nobody will know the difference, anyway.

Here is a sample profile I have made for guidance:

Hi! My name is Thomas Brooks and I'm a full time graphics designer and artist, living and working in LA. I've been painting for 12 years and love creating icons and graphics for websites, eBook covers and more. Here on Fiverr, I have already sold more than 600 gigs.

You can send me a message any time or find me at [your website or social media profile].

Now obviously, you can't talk about how many orders you have already completed when you're just starting out. But once you are more experienced and have a number of satisfied customers, it's definitely beneficial to mention it!

Here's a different kind of profile:

*My name is Thomas Brooks and I offer the cheapest and most professional icons and eBook covers on fiverr.com * More than 600 sales * 100% Reputation * Fast Response Time * Great Customer Care. Improve your media with BrooksDesign!*

This profile is shaped more like an advertisement, listing the benefits and calling the reader to action at the end. The username for this profile would be "BrooksDesign". Both of these options are perfectly fine, but my personal preference is the first one, because it feels much more warm, alive and real to me. It has the same effect as showing your face to your customers and allows them to bond a little bit with the person behind that profile. You need to decide for yourself what you want to do and what feels right for the kind of services you wish to provide. If you don't intend to go into a specific direction but have gigs of all colors and sizes, then just be general and go with the first option, since it's hard to have a profile shaped like an advertisement if you don't specialize.

Gig Creation in a Nutshell

Now that we have a decent profile page and are armed with the 6 pillars, we are ready to learn how to create our first gig. The process of doing so used to be very simple with the old design of the website; not it is even simpler. In order to create a gig, go to the Fiverr homepage and click on "SALES" at the top bar of the page. Then click on "Create Gig" on the right.

You will be taken to the gig creation form, where you can specify everything. Choose a title and category for your gig that matches it best. This is to make sure the moderators approve it and potential customers are able to find it. Next, write down the description of your gig; you can write up to 1200 symbols.

Whenever somebody orders your gig, they get an automated message which you are going to specify in the text box below the description. No matter what your gig is about, your customer usually has to provide you with some information for you to get started. This could be just some text, a description of their wish for an eBook cover, a photo, or perhaps a video or audio file. The order will only become active, that is the clock will start ticking, once they have responded to this automated message. Lastly, write down some keywords that best describe your gig. If someone uses one of your keywords in the search function, they will be able to find your gig. The best thing to do here is to use words that are also used the title.

Next, specify how many days you are going to need to complete the order. In the beginning you will have more time for lack of orders, so choose a smaller time span to attract customers, but make sure you deliver on time. If you don't deliver on time your customer is able to cancel the order and will give you a negative review. Once you get more orders it's advisable to raise the time span so you can get everything done.

Upload images you have found or created for your gig by clicking on the "browse" button. Once you are a level 1 seller on Fiverr, you will have access to the "Gig Extras" function where you can offer additions to your gig for an extra fee. People can then order your normal gig and optionally choose to get the extra as well. Choose how long it'll take you to complete the Gig Extra and that amount of time will be added to the overall time for the whole order.

So if you choose three days for the main gig and two days for the extra, you'll have five days to complete the order. At the end, activate the checkbox if the result of your work is something that has to be shipped and click on the "Save" button.

Video-fy your Gig and get more sales.

Did you know that sellers who present their service on video, sell 220% more?

Something is still missing – the video! This is very important.

You can use animoto.com, or film yourself and talk into the camera. People respond very well to personal communications. If you are unsure of what kind of video to upload, just look at some high ranking gigs for ideas.

How to Deal With Customers

Six Things to Remember

1 - Always be polite and courteous to your customer.

2 - If they are rude, simply ignore it and continue to satisfy point 1.

3 - Make your customer feel important.

4 - Your customer always comes first.

5 - Answer their questions. No question is too silly to answer.

6 - Watch your language; don't talk like a gangsta rapper or slacker.

How to Avoid Negative Reviews

Have you ever noticed that any YouTube video with a decent number of views has at least one negative vote? Some people are negative by nature, while others are impossible to please, even if your work is impeccable. I believe the only way to deal with a customer like this is to offer to revise your work until they're satisfied. Whenever you deliver your work, a forced message exchange takes place. Put something like this at the end of the message:

I want to make sure you are perfectly satisfied with my work, so please let me know if something is not to your liking before you place your review!

I've never gotten a negative review in all my time on Fiverr, and ever since I've told some of my friends to implement this policy and provide valuable customer service, they haven't gotten a single negative review either. And that's true even for customers who first hated either our work.

However, some people will actually go so far as to blackmail you to do more work than you agreed to, threatening you to give you a negative review if you don't comply. If something like this happens, copy the conversation between you and your customer, go to the Fiverr support and report that abusive user. Fiverr has a fantastic support staff! They are very helpful, very fast to respond and very nice. I can't tell what their response would be, since I've never had this situation, but it's the only right action to take. I only mention this because I recently saw someone on Warrior Forum who had been blackmailed in this way and failed to ask the support for help. Instead, he went along with the demands of that customer in order to preserve his pristine review statistics.

Reputation is what it's all about – never forget that. Sometimes I couldn't care less about a customer, namely if they're just rude or talk to you as though they are plain stupid. Some people are weird or have a problem communicating with other people. But you must never allow yourself to treat them the way they treat you. Smile to yourself and you'll feel better, then go on.

Instruction Message Blueprint

Whenever someone orders to gig, they get an automated message that you have to specify. In general, this message contains instructions from your end that your customer has to respond to. Here's how you could word your instruction message:

"Hello and thank you for your order!

Please provide me with the following things, so I can start working right away

1) ….

2) ….

3) ….

Kind regards,

Signature"

It's important to greet you customer, to thank them and to be polite in asking for needed information. Should you only need one kind of information, simply make it a part of the second sentence, such as: *"please provide me with the URL to your website, so I can promote it to my Twitter followers right away"*

Remember that a gig only begins once your customer responds to this automated message. If you have a customer who orders your gig multiple times but only responds to one of those messages, politely explain to them why they have to respond to each message. It doesn't matter what they write as long as they write something.

Order Completion Message Blueprint

Another forced message exchange takes place at the completion of an order. When this occurs, you should again be professional about what you write and better don't make something up on the spot. Here is a message template I've used myself:

Hello/Good day/Hi [Customer Username],

I've (successfully) completed your order and have attached your article/review/video/etc

If you need my services again, feel free to return anytime. (Perhaps you would be interested in a related premium service I provide. It goes beyond ordinary Fiverr gigs and can be found here [your website].)

I wish to make sure you are completely satisfied with my work, so please let me know if something is not to your liking before you place your review!

On the other hand, if you feel my work is worth more than five dollars, feel free to tip me here if you wish: [Link to tip gig]. (See Obolus Maximus gig in section 2)

Kind regards,

Signature

With such a message at the end, recurring customers are almost guaranteed. No matter how you customize this template or if you create your own, make sure you have a greeting, an announcement that you have completed the older, an invitation to come again, a customer service line and a tip line at the end. I know, this doesn't leave much room for change. Don't fix what ain't broken, I suppose.

Take Action

If you have an ordinary job, you have the "comfort" of a clear schedule. You get up in the morning at a certain time, go to the office or wherever you may work and your superior tells you what to do until it's time to go home. Perhaps you even take some of your work home with you. However, if you have a business or are in the process of building one, then you are your own boss, have to create your own schedule and take action yourself.

Having to take action yourself and consciously act against your own, natural sluggishness is one of the biggest problems for people when it's about making money online. This is a calamity very common among beginners, as they find it very hard to focus and actually use the materials or tools they buy.

Making money online isn't rocket science; trust me, one of us has actually *done* rocket science. Internet marketing (and making money online in general) is substantially simpler than most people think. More precisely, it's simple but not easy, meaning it requires work. All the people that have success online have taken massive action and implement the things they learn. They are not afraid to make mistakes and grow from those mistakes. One of the biggest mistakes you can make is to continue to read, dream and imagine what it'd be like to be successful instead of taking action and getting there. And that's true for beginners as well as experienced marketers, for I have seen this problem manifest itself in both of them

You don't need to create 20 gigs right away – in fact you shouldn't. It's perfectly fine to start with two or three and get used to working on Fiverr before you add more gigs. If you have too many gigs in the beginning, you might get overwhelmed while you are still learning to use the platform. Also take into account that you'll have to devote time to complete the orders you get. Bring it slowly into your daily routine to make it fit – but not too slowly!

It's equally important not to get confused by the number of possibilities presented here. Don't spend too much time trying to weigh the options of which gig idea to use. Simply pick any two or three you feel you can do and focus on that for a while.

When we humans are presented with a whole lot of choice, we have trouble choosing and tend not to choose at all. To psychologists this is known as the Choice Overload Problem. Be aware of this human flaw, so that you can remember it if you find yourself at a loss, trying to choose out of all those possibilities. Instead, choose not to be confused; just go with two or three of these gigs and be done with choosing. As long as you can complete your orders, it doesn't really matter what you do.

I urge you to follow my lead and take the plunge. Just do it!

Now, let's get into the thick of things and talk about the gigs themselves.

The Gig Treasure Chest

Welcome inside the Gig Treasure Chest! In this section I'll unlock a whirl of creativity, great and clever ideas and a lot of tricks and techniques for you. All of the contents in my treasure chest have been tested not just by me, but also by all my friends whom I've helped to find success on Fiverr.

In order to keep things organized I've divided all of the individual gigs into categories, depending on the time it takes to complete them and their difficulty rating, which has been carefully chosen by me under consideration of the input from my friends and their own experience. I'm going to describe each gig and break them down into actionable steps.

You'll find more ideas than you can implement, given that you can only have up to 20 gigs in one account, and creating the second, third or even more accounts is frowned on by Fiverr. Actually, you can only have 19 gigs, because there is one which is absolutely obligatory, as you're about to see…

Obligatory: The Obolus Maximus

No matter what kind of gigs you end up doing, this one is obligatory for you to have in your gig repertoire! It's so simple and yet most people never come to the idea: give your customers a chance to tip you.

That's right! You should have a gig that simply says: *"I will humbly accept a tip for $5"*.

Imagine you have done great work, completed your order early and even over delivered. Your customer is very happy with the result and perhaps even amazed to get something like this for just $5. By offering them a way to give you a tip, they might feel compelled to do so, especially if the work we have done was indeed very good. A lot of people feel bad to ignore this option, perhaps thinking they have exploited you or are ungrateful if they don't give you tip. So they go ahead.

Whenever you complete an order, you are forced by Fiverr to send a message to your customer. At the end of this message, you should always attach a text like this:

"I always do what I can to deliver. If you feel my work is worth more than five dollars, please feel free to tip me here: [Link to your tip gig]"

If you want to really crush it, you can add a heartwarming detail such as:

"All the tips I get are going to be used for the birthday of my little sister."

I would advise you not to use the exact same line, otherwise a lot of people might be using it soon and make it less believable. Whether lying to people is okay with you or not is entirely up to you. Personally, I use a story much like this one and it's the truth. If it weren't, I wouldn't use it, because that's not how I am.

To get the best effect, use a sweet smiley, a heart with a "thank you" on it, or some other heartwarming image for your Obolus Maximus gig.

Easy Gigs

Easy Gig 1 | The Proofreader

Possible gig titles: *I will professionally proof-read up to 500 words by hand for $5*

I will professionally proof-read your CV by hand for $5

Time per order: A few minutes

This is one of the easiest gigs imaginable, and yet it produces enormous results. People will give you their CVs, articles for websites, websites themselves and rarely even whole books to be checked for errors. There is so much written content in the world, and especially on the Internet, that proofreading is an evergreen way to make money and always in high demand. In order to be competitive, simply raise the number of words you offer to proofread if necessary.

Of course, we aren't going to do the work by hand, since there's a lot of software out there specifically programmed to check for grammatical errors. It is, however, inadvisable to use spellcheckers, because they're generally not capable of correcting grammar.

Manual

1 - Go to the order on Fiverr and download the text your customer provided you with.

2 - Go to either of these websites. These are the best grammar checkers I know of, but they aren't free to use. Luckily, you can test them for free and that is all we need.

www.gingersoftware.com

www.whitesmoke.com

www.grammarly.com

If you want to use free software, I get the best results with paperrater, plus the site is very easy to use. Many others I've tried don't even find ordinary spelling mistakes if I put them in intentionally.

<u>**www.paperrater.com**</u>

Since new sites like these can pop up all the time, feel free to Google for "grammar checker" or something similar. You should come across the first three I mentioned right away. There are a lot of alternatives. Of course, you can also use MS Word, but it isn't quite perfect.

3 - With the results from the software, correct the text, go back to Fiverr and send the result to your customer. Don't forget to include the line for your Obolus Maximus gig!

Easy Gig 2 | The Geyserist

Possible gig title: *I will turn your website into a professional Android app for $5*

Time per order: A few minutes

Smartphones are everywhere nowadays, so we should tap into this development and make a hefty profit from it. In this gig we're going to turn websites into Android apps, which is something that sells far more often than you would think. You can easily get a few hundred orders with this gig. Best of all, completing an order will only take you about 2 minutes and it's completely free!

In the automated message you send to your customers, tell them you need the URL of the website, a short description of your website, a category and a name for the application.

Manual

1 - Go to the order page on Fiverr and get the data you need from your customer.

2 - Go to the website **www.appsgeyser.com** and sign up for a free account, if this is the first time you use it.

3 - Click on the "create now!" button on the homepage and fill in the website URL, App name, category and short description. You can leave the rest the way it is. When you're done click on "create".

4 - Go to your dashboard, select the application in the drop-down menu at the top and click on the "test" button. You are directed to a new page where you can download the app and its QR code.

5 - Put the file and the code in a zip archive and send it to your customer on Fiverr.

Be aware of it that appsgeyser puts small banner ads on the websites generated this way, but I've never had anyone complain about it.

With a little bit of research and more websites like appsgeyser popping up all over the Internet, it should be no problem for you to extend this method to other types of smartphones such as the iPhone. I'm sure there are also ways to create apps like this with no advertisement on them. One of these options is to use the android app inventor, which at the time of writing this has become open source.

As a general piece of advice, the mobile market is growing intensely and represents a great number of opportunities to make money. If you are creative, I'm sure you can come up with many ways to do little things like this and sell it as a service on Fiverr.

Easy Gig 3 | The Card Designer

Possible gig title: *I will create 3 PROFESSIONAL business cards for you for $5*

Time per order: 5 minutes

Nowadays, everybody and their grandma needs a business card. This gig is another evergreen way to make money and it's very competitive, because a lot of people do it. But the wonderful thing is, it's very simple to create a business card like the one on the right. It took me only about 2 minutes to do it. We can easily offer to create a set of these cards to be more competitive. Your customers will love to get several cards so they can choose the one they like best. By doing this, your sales, positive reviews and the likelihood to get a tip will increase.

Another way to be more competitive is to create multiple gigs with different titles and slightly different offers, thereby increasing the chances for someone to find one of your gigs.

There are two ways to create these cards fast.

One entails doing it by hand, the other by software. Before you begin, go to Google, search for "free business card templates" and download as many templates as you can find.

Manual

1 - Go to the order page on Fiverr and see if your customer has provided you with any specifications on what the card should look like. Copy all of this data to put it on the card itself.

2 - If you go with the manual option, pick a template that matches your customer's needs and open it up in a program so you can change the text on it. What program you need to use depends on what kind of format the template file has. If possible, I recommend using Adobe Photoshop. For a free solution, you can use **GIMP**.

3 - You can also automate the whole thing by going to **www.businesscardland.com**, where you can choose from a number of designs, type in the data, create the card with the push of a button and change the colors in case you want or need to.

4 - Safe the cards as JPEG files, put them into a zip archive, go back to Fiverr and send it to your customer.

5 - It may be your customer wants the original editable files, like the Photoshop files. In that case, try to get another order out of them for the template, or offer it as a $5 addition to your gig once you are a level 1 seller.

6 - Don't forget to ask for your tip!

Easy Gig 4 | The Video to Audio Wiz

Possible gig titles: *I will convert a video into an mp3 file for $5*

I will convert a music video into an audio file for $5

Time per order: 3-5 minutes

Welcome to the easiest gig in all of the universe, but remarkably, it sells like bottles of water in the Sahara. A great number of people go to YouTube to find music videos, and the same amount of people would very much like to keep the music from those videos to put it on their phone or MP3 player.

Most people don't know how to download a video from YouTube in the first place, so there are two missing bits of knowledge that keep people from doing this gig themselves. First, they don't know how to get the videos onto their hard drive, and secondly, they don't know how to grab the audio from said video and turn it into an MP3 and other audio format. Of course, our gig will be more general than just turning YouTube music videos into music; this is just an example of a common motivation for people to order your gig, and something you can advertise in your description.

It might be that you get a video from a customer, or that you have to grab it first.

Manual

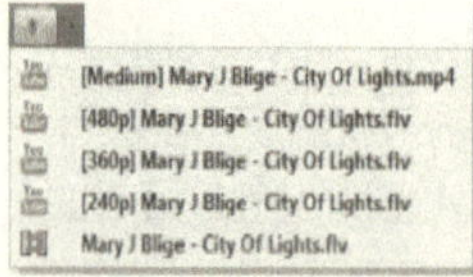

1 - Open up Firefox and download the **download helper** add-on. It will add an icon in your browser by which you can grab videos, audio and flash files from websites that don't have a download button.

2 - The icon is grayed out if there is no video available on the website you're currently visiting. When you are on a video streaming site such as YouTube, the icon becomes active. Click on the little arrow next to it and choose the best quality video for download. Here, it's [480p].

3 - You can use free software such as the **xilisoft video to audio converter** to extract the audio from the video. Now just sent the result your customer.

4 - Don't forget to ask for your tip!

I described it like this because using the software makes you versatile. However, the process of grabbing a video from YouTube and saving us an audio file can be done far simpler and faster. All you need to do is go to **www.youtube-mp3.org** copy-and-paste the YouTube URL, hit the button and you're done.

Easy Gig 5 | The Information Broker (100s of Gigs in One)

Possible gig titles: *I will sell you a beginner's guide to [topic] for $5*

Concrete example: *I will send you a beginner's eBook on how to care for your fish for $5*

Time per order: After setup, 10 seconds

Note: This is 100s of gigs in one.

In this gig we're going to sell info eBooks. If there's one thing people are always looking to get on the Internet, it's information – and that as quickly as possible. We are going to offer it to them, therefore saving them the work to find and assemble it themselves. Information sells very easily, and information written by the masters, who really know what they're talking about, sells even better.

In principle, you can offer hundreds of guides on Fiverr and – unlike me – you don't even have to write them yourself. General topics such as "dog training" have been covered by many people before you, so the information is readily available on the Internet. Make sure you use the word "beginner's" in the title of your gig; this is to make sure that your customer won't expect more and end up disappointed. In order to increase the value of your gig and get more sales, offer a money back guarantee, if your customers aren't satisfied.

The magical words are "Master Resell Rights" (MRR) or "Private Label Rights" (PLR).

Manual

1 - Go to **exclusiveniche.com**, **thePLRstore.com** or **tidbit.com**; you will find hundreds of eBooks ready for download. Ordinarily you have to buy them, but they are very cheap and often come in packages of dozens or even hundreds.

2 - Keep in mind that guides on how to care for animals are very popular, because a lot of people have pets and need to learn how to care for them. Once you find something that looks promising to you, buy and save the package on your hard drive.

3 - Create a gig for every book you think has potential to sell – if you have a package of books on one topic, you can increase the value of your gig by offering either the whole package or a selection of it. The nice thing about PLR products is that you can change and recombine them, stick your name on them and sell them as your own. In principle, you can make an account on Fiverr where you just sell these eBooks.

4 - After this process, every order can be completed in a few seconds, since

you only have to send the book(s) to your customer.

5 - Don't forget to ask for your tip!

Easy Gig 6 | The Dictation Man

Possible gig titles: *I will transcribe up to 5 minutes of Audio for you for $5*

Time per order: 2 - 5 minutes

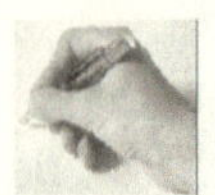

It's not entirely clear to me why, but it turns out a whole lot of people need audio tracks transcribed. In case you don't know what a transcription is, it simply means you get an audio file of people speaking, and you are supposed to write down what they say.

If English is your main language, or if you have no problem understanding spoken English even if people have an accent, this gig is child's play.

As always, be competitive by offering to transcribe a longer audio track than your competitors. But even if you offer a shorter amount of time, you'll still get orders, because not everybody needs to transcribe a long audio track. If you look more professional, people are likely to go with your service even if you offer to transcribe a shorter audio track than others. If a customer has a long track to transcribe, they might test you first and then give you multiple orders to do more. Once you are a level 1 seller and can offer additions to your gig, you could offer to transcribe 15 more minutes of audio for additional $10, thus giving them 5 minutes for free.

Manual

1 - Go to your order page on Fiverr and download the audio file your customer sent you.

2 - Open the audio file in an audio editing software such as Adobe Audition, or **Audacity**. I recommend audacity, because it's free and not as complicated to use.

3 - Slow down the audio track by going to the "effects" tab and select "change tempo". By doing this, it's way easier to understand what the people are saying, especially if they talk fast.

4 - Write down each sentence in a Word or **Open Office** document. If there is

more than one person talking, label the people as "Man 1, Man 2, Woman 1" or something like that. Whenever someone else starts speaking, make a new line. The result should essentially look like the text in the chat room.

5 - Save your document in a format everybody can open, such as a *.txt file. Go back to Fiverr and send the result to your customer. If you're unable to understand what the people are saying, ask your customer if it's fine if parts of the transcription are blank.

6 - If you manage to get everything right, don't forget to ask for your tip!

Easy Gig 7 | The Wholesale Broker

Possible gig titles: *I will send you a list of 8,000 wholesale suppliers for $5*

I will send you a list of 400 eBay friendly wholesale suppliers for $5

Time per order: 10-15 minutes to set up, then 10 seconds.

With websites such as eBay or Amazon, everybody is able to sell items on the Internet. One of the best ways to make money by selling items is to buy them from a wholesale supplier and then put them on eBay or open up an Amazon shop. If done right, even beginners can make a decent amount of money this way, if they only knew where to get these items in the first place.

Selling lists of wholesale suppliers, especially eBay friendly wholesale suppliers and drop shippers, is a fairly good performing gig for something that only requires you to send a list. It isn't a top seller anymore, but very easy money that adds to the results of your other gigs.

Remember, the people who really profited from the gold rush were not the poor men digging for gold, but the smart men selling the tools to dig for gold. Wholesale lists are in high demand, and so we are going to tap into it. Since there is a lot of competition for this sort of gig, it helps to create many of them. If you have several accounts, you could for example create two or three per account.

Manual

1 - Head over to Google and search for "free wholesale list".

2 - When you're looking for a list, make sure it's not a small one, but contains thousands and thousands of entries. Naturally, you can combine smaller lists into larger ones, though you run the risk of having the same supplier more than once. Given the end result will end up huge, I doubt anyone would ever notice.

3 - Most of the time you can download a list by Torrent or file sharing websites such as hotfile, oron, rapidshare and so on. You can also buy lists, but make sure they come with master resell rights so you're able to resell them legally.

4 - Assemble everything into a zip archive or PDF and you're set.

5 - When you get an order, simply send the zip or PDF to your customer.

6 - It's unlikely to work in this case, but don't forget to ask for your tip!

Easy Gig 8 | The Web Whisperer

Possible gig titles: *I will promote your website to my 10,000 Twitter followers for $5*

I will promote your website to my 10,000 Facebook fans for $5

Time per order: 20 seconds

Here is another one of those very well selling gigs, commonly used in the Internet marketing space. Perhaps you're wondering how in the world you're supposed to get those 10,000+ Twitter followers or Facebook fans to promote to in the first place, but that's not much of a problem, really.

There are people on Fiverr who offer to get you thousands of followers and fans for a single order, so all you have to do is order from a few off them first. Once you have all these followers and fans, you can do these promotion gigs. Of course, the more people you have, the more orders you will get. It has been one of my best-selling gigs and is very much worth it since it doesn't require any time to do it. Whether or not these followers and fans are responsive or not doesn't matter. If most of them are bots doesn't matter either. The only thing that matters is that you have them; that's what people are interested in.

Manual

1 - Head over to Fiverr and search for gigs that give you Twitter followers and Facebook fans. Don't give the people you buy from a review, since your name will otherwise be displayed on their gig and we want to make sure that no one ever notices we got our fans and followers from there.

2 - Once you have at least 5,000 of them, which should happen quickly, create either one or two gigs where you offer to promote whatever your customer wants. If you create one gig, offer to do it in both social networks. If you separate two gigs, then one will be only for Twitter and the other for Facebook. Tell your customer in the automated message that they should provide you with the URL and the message you are supposed to send to your followers and fans, just in case your customer wants to specify it. Otherwise just write something yourself.

3 - When you get an order, go to Fiverr and find out which URL you are supposed to promote and what to say about it.

4 - Go to Twitter and/or Facebook and do the promotion.

5 - Copy the link to the tweet or Facebook message and send it to your customer to complete the order.

6 - Since this is pretty simple, the tip is unlikely to work here. Better don't ask.

Easy Gig 9 | The Ping Pong Man

Possible gig title: *I will submit up to 5 websites, RRS feeds and podcasts to 100+ ping servers, RSS and podcast aggregators to get your sites noticed by the search engines for $5*

Time per order: 5 minutes

This is the kind of gig I like the best, where everything that happens is completely automated and free at the same time. Pinging is a push mechanism by which a weblog notifies the server that its content has been updated. Or, to put it simply: "Hey search engine! I have been updated – look here!"

Whatever you do, you always need to ping your sites whenever there's an update. Most blogging platforms automatically ping one or more servers each time new content is added, or old content is updated. In my experience, few people know about this automation. You can easily sell people your pinging service, as well as the service to add people's RSS feeds to RSS aggregators. Well, this is not a high earning gig, for the simple reason of this being easy to do, but you can still make a couple hundred dollars within a few months from this. There is no reason why you shouldn't have it in your repertoire, just sitting there and waiting to be ordered. All that matters is that it works and makes you extra money. Besides, I haven't seen all that many people doing this.

Manual

1 - Go to Fiverr and copy the URL of the website as well as the RSS and podcast URLs, provided by your customer. Most people won't have all three of these.

2 - Go to

www.pingfarm.com

www.feedshark.brainbliss.com

www.pingler.com

Add all the URLs to the different services and ping them for free.

3 - Return to Fiverr and tell your customer you have completed the work. Whatever happens, never tell them how you do it, even if they ask you to prove you've actually completed the work. Just tell them it's not possible to prove it, if they ask.

4 - Asking for a tip would go a bit too far in this case, so I think it would be best not to mention it. Otherwise it may disgruntle your customer!

Medium Gigs

Medium Gig 1 | The Article Writer

Possible gig titles: *I will write a 500 word SEO optimized original article for $5*

I will write a 500 word original article on any subject for $5

Time per order: 15-20 minutes

Writing articles is a timeless classic among all the outsourcing jobs anyone can do. It's continuously in high demand and with a little bit of practice and the proper software fairly easy to do.

Search engines such as Google are content providing machines, and in order to rank well on them, a webmaster needs good, original content on their website – a whole lot of content. Because of this fact, they usually pay outsourcers like you to write articles for them. While this kind of gig can be a bit tedious and time-consuming, it's certainly something that will bring in a lot of orders and can very well get you started on Fiverr. If you happen to enjoy writing, you can make a lot of money with this gig alone.

Make sure you choose a gig title that offers more words than your competitors, but don't go too far as that'll make it harder and more time-consuming. You can try 500 words and see if you get orders, then try 600 and 700 to test. You might also want to satisfy the Pillar of Initiation by having a catchy title that stands out. You can use words like "professional" or "creative", but I think "SEO optimized" will get you by far the best results. SEO optimized articles have keywords which are repeated very often inside the article, to allow them to rank high in search engines for that keyword. If you want to write an article, you will need to ask your customer to tell you not just the topic but also the keyword or keywords.

What you should also do is advertise any writing experience you have! If you happen to be a part-time writer or studied English, it should be easy to put that into the description and make it sound good and professional. It's safe to say that people like to see that.

I now want to tell you about two ways of how to create arti way relies on want I'm doing right now as I'm writing this eBook. I'm not typing on my keyboard most of the time! What I'm really doing is speaking into my microphone. Nowadays, speech-to-text technology has advanced to level where it's actually possible to speak to your computer and have your speech turn into text with minimal errors. I use *Dragon Naturally Speaking* for this task, as do many other successful article writers. You can talk much faster than you can type, and it's even more comfortable. All you have to do is a little bit of research and tell your computer what to write.

While Dragon NaturallySpeaking may be paid software, I can assure you it's extremely worth the price. Writing these lines only requires me to think and to speak clearly into the microphone of my headset, sometimes correcting when either the software makes a mistake or I pronounce something badly. All the time while I'm speaking, the software learns how I speak, and every time I correct something it learns as well. In addition, there are many training modules that allow you to train the software so that it understands your voice and the way you speak. Writing this entire paragraph took me only about a minute.

Manual

1 - Go to an article directory like Ezine articles, Wikipedia or to other sources of information to study the topic you are supposed to write an article about. Note: Never steal articles!

2 - Either use Dragon NaturallySpeaking or your keyboard to produce an original article from what you learned from the source material.

3 - Obviously, you need to give the result a grammar and spell check, using the tools presented in the Spell Master gig (Easy Gig 1).

4 - Finally, do what you can to incorporate any keywords your customer has specified for the article.

5 - Go back to Fiverr and sent the article to your customer.

Optionally, you can use the next gig as an addition to this one to catch two orders from one customer. If the customer orders many articles from you, which is likely to happen, they may also order the addition every time.

Medium Gig 2 | The Article Translator

Possible gig title: *I will translate up to 500 words into [LANGUAGE] for $5*
Time per order: 15 - 20 minutes

It may not seem that way to you, but I made a killing with this gig. Remember what I said in the last gig about how all webmasters need content for their websites to rank well in the search engines? Imagine you were to offer them to translate either the article you have written for them or any text they want into a foreign language! By combining the article writing with the translation gig, you can sometimes get both from the same customer. In order to be able to do this gig you **must** speak that language; there is no way to create a correct translation automatically. Even today there is no software capable of understanding language well enough to translate a text flawlessly. However, we are still going to use software to make the process easier.

German, French, Spanish, Italian and other European languages are hot and sell. I've got no experience with Asian languages, so if you are Asian, you'll have to test the demand yourself.

Manual

1 - Go to Fiverr and copy the text or download the text file your customer sent you.

2 - Go to the **Google translator tool**, choose the source and target language and paste the text into the text box.

3 - Open up a two Word documents or Open Office files, position them right next to each other on your screen, then copy and paste the flawed result from the translator into one of them. Now copy the original text into the other file to enable you to look at both of them the same time.

4 - Go over the flawed translation and correct wherever necessary. Be prepared for nonsensical sentences. By having the original version available, you'll always be able to see what something was *supposed* to mean.

Sometimes the translation works for a whole paragraph, or individual sentences. Parts of sentences are usually correct. Another bonus you get by using the translator is that words or phrases you don't know are usually translated accurately. All of this saves you a lot of time, but under no circumstances should you ever use only the translator and try to fool your customer, because it's not right and a lot of my customers were actually from the target language, meaning they would've noticed immediately. I even had customers who tested me by using an article before giving me a larger task. I once translated an entire business website for a customer, which were 16 orders at once.

5 - When you're done, go back to Fiverr and send the text to your customer.

Medium Gig 3 | The Logo Designer

Possible gig titles: *I will create an AWESOME logo for you for $5*

I will make 3 CREATIVE logos for you for $5

Time per order: 10-15 minutes

 A lot of people have use for a logo, be it for a website, an eBook or a mobile app. It takes a while to get used to completing this task and doing it quickly, but if you're artistic, it should be very easy for you to pick up.

We have two possibilities for creating logos. You can either create a logo in Photoshop or any other program of your choice by hand, or we can use a tool specifically designed for logo creation. If you are artistically minded, actually know how to paint and want to go with the first option, you should create one awesome logo like the one I show here. I don't recommend using this as your main gig, because it's way too time-consuming. For the second option, you should offer to create several logos in order to be competitive.

Since such a logo is worth more than $5, this gig can easily get you a tip from your customer, so your income is often $8 instead of $4. Once you are a level 1 seller and can offer additions, you could offer the first option for $20 or so, if you are able to paint.

If you really want to crush it with this gig, offer a free revision, in case your customer wants something on their logo to be changed. They will be more likely to order from you, if they have that assurance and, of course, be even more likely to tip you!

Manual

1 - Go to the order page on Fiverr and see if your customer said anything about what the logo should be like.

2 - Go to **www.logomaker.com** for the free solution or to **www.aaa-logo.com** for the paid solution. You can also go to Google and look for "free logo designer" or "free logo creator" if you aren't happy with these options. Software like this comes with templates and a whole lot of graphics you can use and combine to create logos.

3 - If you use the software the first time, it should only take you a few minutes of playing around to get used to it, and the more you use it, the faster you will be able to make these logos in the future. Now create the logos and save them. If you use the paid solution, be sure to save the projects as well. After all, you might be able to use the same logos or slightly different versions of them for somebody else.

4 - Put your logos in a zip file, go to Fiverr and send it to your customer.

5 - If your customer wants you to change something, do it and be done with it.

6 - Don't forget to ask for your tip!

Medium Gig 4 | The Teacher (100s of Gigs in One)

Possible gig titles: *I will teach you how to [topic] for $5*

Concrete example:*I will teach you how to get unlimited Twitter followers for $5*

Time per order: Depends on what you do

Note: This is 100s of gigs in one.

In this gig were going to sell our knowledge of a certain topic, or a simple trick that's valuable to a lot of people. This gig is very much like the Information Broker (Easy Gig 5), except that we are going to create the information ourselves. We can create a small eBook or film the video where we explain something of great value to our customer. If you know a lot about SEO or backlinking in order to get people's website ranked in Google, you could teach them that. But what most people really want to know is how to get Facebook likes or YouTube views themselves, so you can tell them that secret. Only do that if you don't want to sell them the likes and views yourself. I reveal how to do that in Section 3 of this guide.

Another thing you can do is help people with math or some other tutoring job like that. Seriously, there's bound to be something you know or are proficient at that's helpful to people and can be monetized. If you are a mechanic, you can offer advice to someone who has a problem with their car. If you are fluent in a foreign language, you can offer to teach people over Skype for 20 minutes per order, so that an hour would be three orders, or $12.

Manual

1 - For eBooks, open up MS Word or get yourself **Open Office**, which is free. When you're done writing, simply save it as a PDF file.

2 - If you want to create a video, you can either use your camera or use a screen capture software such as Camtasia, which is the best on the market and what I use myself.

3 - Send your eBook to your customer, or upload your video to MediaFire and send them the download link.

4 - Don't forget to ask for your tip!

Medium Gig 5 | The Offliner

Possible gig title: *I will post 50 flyers in a major US city to advertise your website for $5*

Time per order: 10-15 minutes

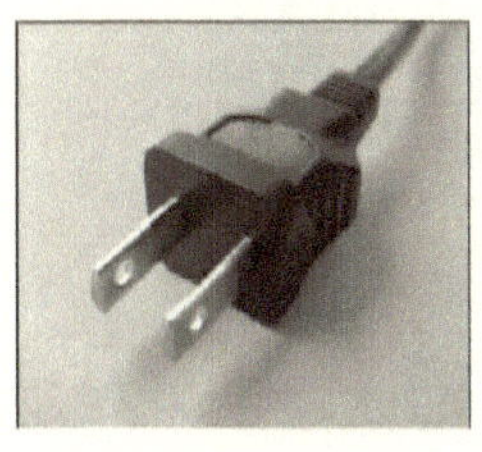

There are still lots of people who like offline marketing. And I'm not at all talking about old-fashioned people, but Internet marketers! Most of the Internet marketing millionaires I know have done offline marketing before or still do it for some of their online campaigns.

Naturally, this gig depends on where you live, but I've seen a gig from someone in Estonia who has gotten a handful of orders. If you live in or near a major US city, getting orders for your gig should be no problem at all. What's more, I haven't seen a single gig like this with a video in it, and since it's mandatory for us to use a video, you'll stand out immediately. Maybe you're thinking this is going to take too much time. I assure you it won't! Once you are a level 1 seller, you can offer to design the flyers yourself for an extra $10. This is the only thing that might take a bit, but you can potentially get $12 and really profit from every order that includes the addition. You can even offer a second addition for $15, where you offer to design the flyer and provide your customer with the editable Photoshop file of it.

Choose 3 or 4 days as the time you need to complete an order. By doing it this way, you can accumulate several orders and then do them all at once. This is how you save the time.

Manual

1 - Go to Google and search for "free flyer templates" or "free flyer templates psd" to get exactly that. A PSD is an editable Photoshop file. Now put the text on the template, perhaps change a picture or whatever you like, using pictures you find on Google or stock websites.

2 - Print out 4 flyers per page in order to save ink and paper.

3 - Take your camera or mobile phone, go to the cafeteria of your local

university and put the flyers around the tables. At my local university, something like this is done every day, and it's so large that 50 flyers aren't even nearly enough to fill the room. You can also go to a densely populated location and give the flyers away, but that will take much longer and is tedious. Take pictures of the flyers on the tables as proof.

4 - Don't forget to ask for your tip!

Medium Gig 6 | The Cover Artist

Possible gig titles: *I will design an AWESOME eBook, DVD or Boxshot cover for $5*

Time per order: 10-15 minutes

I urge you to pay very close attention now, because this is one of the best-selling gigs of all time and is unlikely to ever stop being that. In general, Internet marketing related gigs have the highest amount of interest and therefore sell the most. Naturally, this also means you have a massive amount of competition, but it's fairly easy to create fantastic covers. I just created the one on the right in 1 minute, without even trying.

How is this possible, you ask? Simple, there is software out there specifically designed for this task. It allows you to choose a base, such as these booklets here, and add a background, text and graphics from an archive. If you want to, you can also use your own graphics and background. The best part is that your customers will provide the background images themselves! So you select it, click a button and your design is put onto the base as though it's always been there. There's no need for Photoshop or other complicated software at all. It all happens in the browser.

It's imperative you use the image spaces on your gig description page to showcase a whole lot of these designs. Since you only have three spaces for images, use graphics software like Photoshop to put a set of these designs into one picture in order to show more of them. This will look very impressive to your potential customers. For your video slideshow, also use a bunch of these designs to show them.

I don't recommend using free software for this, because the competition is steep. Paid software produces better results, comes with an extensive graphics archive and is generally more versatile than free solutions. In addition, free solutions are typically trials with worse performance. If you concentrate on cover creation, you can potentially get thousands of orders, so paid software is utterly worth it. Another wonderful aspect of this gig is that you will get lots of recurring customers!

Manual

1 - Personally, we've been using **this solution** for a long time, as do most of the other successful people who offer the service.

2 - Design the cover or covers, if you choose to offer more than one to your customer to stand out from the crowd.

3 - When you're done, export the results and save them in a zip archive.

4 - Send the results to your customer and don't forget to ask for your tip, which in this case may very well happen, if you truly deliver.

Medium Gig 7 | The Holy Man

Possible gig titles: *I will meditate on your financial abundance or love life for $5*

I will make a wish come true for $5

I will send you positive energy for $5

I will dispel any curse resting on you for $5

Time per order: None or 10 minutes, depending on preference.

There are many people in the world, particularly in the US, who strongly believe in the spiritual and metaphysical. In this gig, we are going to give these people exactly what they want.

As you can see from the possible gig titles I've listed, each of these gigs requires no work at all, since you don't have to send your customers anything back. I think it's safe to say all psychics in the world are either charlatans or have convinced themselves that what they're doing actually works. Whether you go ahead and actually meditate on someone else's financial abundance, send someone positive energy or dispel curses, or simply tell them you have done so doesn't matter. What matters is that it gives these people hope and a feeling of security, which is what they crave. However, if you happen to be someone who actually does meditate and is deeply involved in these sorts of things, you are in a position do these gigs properly, if you choose to.

Believe it or not, these gigs get ordered at least in the dozens, some I've seen with over 100, even several hundred reviews. And that means they get ordered even more often, since not everybody posts these reviews. Believers will return, so you may very well have recurring customers. What's more, you **will** get tips for this service. You should always give your customers some advice on the way for extra value and to uphold the illusion of the deeply involved holy person, monk or whatever sitting on the other end.

Another thing you can do is astrology, essentially giving someone their horoscope, which is something you can create for free on the Internet and even by using software. Actually, you can just make something up in good astrologer fashion. If you want to get into this, go to Google and look for "free horoscope creator" or "astrology software". I've never done this, but I know it works. People who deeply believe in these things generally aren't skeptical and have a strong tendency to believe you. Whether or not it agrees with you to fool people is up to you. It doesn't with me, mind you. All I'm telling you here is that I know it works.

Make sure your gigs show warm pictures of hearts, symbolism of luck and fortune, and a person praying with candles all over the place. If you create a video that represents this, even featuring some meditation music, you should be able to get a lot of orders. It's more like a whole gig campaign and requires an account for itself, since gigs of another nature don't fit very well into such a profile. Just imagine someone looked into your profile and saw a gig related to Internet marketing next to the spiritual ones…

Special Gig – The Invisible Salesman

Welcome to the world of reselling that which others give away cheaply, unknowing how much potential it has and how much money they could make from it. Believe it or not, there are people on Fiverr who sell physical, handmade items. When I first saw it, I stared at my screen for several minutes. Sometimes I forget that most people aren't marketers, don't think like marketers do and don't realize the potential right in front of their eyes.

What we're going to do here is actually not a gig. Instead, we are going to be the ones who order gigs from other sellers and then resell their service for more money to other people outside of Fiverr. And the wonderful thing is: there are many services on Fiverr that can be resold and monetized in a number of ways, making this method versatile and resilient. It's not bound to one gig or one idea, but utilizes a great number of ideas all in the same way.

Option 1

We're going to resell items from Fiverr on eBay.

There may be two barriers in your mind right now. First, you might say that paying $5 for the item on Fiverr, paying for shipping *and* paying eBay fees doesn't sound profitable. And then, you still need to send the item to your customer, which requires physical work and time. Secondly, you might say that you don't live in the United States, which complicates things even further, since the item would have to be shipped to your country. This costs more time and a larger shipping fee, especially since you'd have to send the item somewhere else after getting it. All of this is what keeps people from even coming up with this idea.

I agree that it'd be ridiculous to do the above. What's really going to happen is this: you put the item on eBay.com without even having it in your hand. You can sell an item for more money than it costs on Fiverr. In addition, the customer on eBay also has to pay the shipping fee you specify. Once the auction is over, you place an order for the item on Fiverr and send the seller the customer information of the person who bought the item on eBay. Now the magic happens: Fiverr sellers ship their merchandise without extra fees, because all gigs are supposed to have the fixed price of $5.

Imagine yourself selling a self-made ring for $15 plus $4 shipping fee on eBay. Now you simply order the ring from the seller on Fiverr, tell them where to send it to and lean back as they do the work. Your profit would be $14 minus the eBay fee, and that pretty much without having to do anything at all but put up the auction on eBay and communicate for a minute. Better still, you can sell such an item dozens of times. And since it goes directly from an American seller to an American customer, it doesn't matter where you live. I'm sure you understand the potential, especially if you think about just how many different items are being sold on Fiverr. You can even leverage link building, YouTube views or Twitter follower gigs and offer the same service on eBay for more money, which is something a lot of people offer already. You don't need to know how to do this yourself, if you can just commission it from someone who does. Handcrafted items are better, of course, because they're original and offered by no one else. Also, you get a shipping fee to keep.

Other item info

Item number: 280767520925
Item location: China, China
Ships to: Worldwide See exclusions
Payments: PayPal, Bill Me Later See details
History: 25 sold ⟵

To find something to sell, search for the keyword "handmade" and you'll get gigs where people sell all kinds of self-made items, like rings, necklaces or dolls. When you have found something that seems good, head over to **eBay.com** and search for similar items. Open some of the auctions and look on the right to see how often the item has been sold so far. This gives you a good idea of how popular it is and what's possible for your item. If put up an auction and the item doesn't sell, you don't have to pay any fees as long as you started bidding at $1. Thanks to this, you can test items. Even if something sells only 20 times, this could very well mean $200 or $300 in your pocket.

Option 2

Instead of going with option one and selling the items on eBay, you can create a website and sell the item directly from there. I don't recommend doing that, because gigs can be closed and then your website would become useless, unless you find a way to monetize it in another way. What you can do instead is buy a special type of information, such as a family recipe to make a certain type of cake or some other food. If you really want to crush it, you can contact the seller outside of Fiverr and commission them not just to explain the process, but to create a tutorial for you with photos and perhaps even video as they prepare the food. Once you have all of this in your possession, you can turn the material into a small product, consisting of an eBook, photos and videos. You could even put some of the video material on YouTube to advertise your product and get traffic to your site. A video on how to make a certain type of cake can very well go viral, especially if it's a family recipe. Naturally, you don't want to show the whole process and just have a teaser to get people interested.

This option is essentially a way to leverage Fiverr in terms of creating a niche market product. The necessary information is readily available, just waiting to be found by a clever marketer like you. Fiverr is a gold mine that can be connected to the rest of the Internet and thus combined into other powerful ways to make money. Many people think that doing all this work for other people on Fiverr is tedious and not even proper Internet marketing, but rather just some way to make money online. Nothing could be further from the truth. Don't be blinded by the original function of something! Instead, think about how it could be combined with other things to create something new, which is the basic principle behind invention and progress.

Outlook

The concept of reselling services from Fiverr for more money is powerful and can be twisted in many ways. Be imaginative! For example, you could sell a service about installing and configuring a WordPress blog, as well as doing SEO and link building for it. Create a website to sell this as a service to offline, brick and mortar businesses for $300 or so, when in reality, you get it done by people from Fiverr for much less. Once you have a site that makes a bunch of money this way, you can sell it on **flippa.com** for 10 months' worth of income.

I realize this is all pretty advanced, but I want to have it here to give you a more complete book to work with. Delivering quality to you is important to me. If you are a beginner, you can still come back to this one day.

A Word about Advanced Gigs and Where to Go From Here

Perhaps you're wondering why I don't have a chapter called "Advanced Gigs" here in my treasure chest. First of all, what would qualify as an advanced gig in the first place?

Always remember: Nothing sells as well as gigs related to Internet marketing. An advanced gig must therefore be an advanced Internet marketing related service, capable of producing a large number of sales for preferably a small amount of work.

Do you remember the example I talked about in the introductory chapter, the one about the backlinking gig and my assessment of how much the person behind it was earning? Selling backlinks, building link pyramids and link wheels, and do social bookmarking are indeed the largest gold mines not just on Fiverr, but any other micro worker platform. Every webmaster needs these services to rank their websites; to save time and money, they simply outsource this task for a small price on Fiverr. Once you have more experience, or if you already have this experience and are looking to expand your horizon, getting into backlinking might be the best course of action for you to take as a seller on Fiverr.

Advanced gigs require a bit of an investment, because the software to automate link building and social bookmarking isn't free, but has the potential of enormous returns in the realm of five figures over just a couple of months. Of course, all the other options laid out in this book do also combine to a potential five figure income. But if you want a single gig to produce this much on its own, link building is what you have to look into. Something like that would require its own course, though such software already comes with tutorials, anyway.

Social bookmarking refers to the process of adding a website to all of the social bookmarking platforms out there, thereby helping the added website to rank higher in the search engines. Social bookmarking sites have high authority and page rank, so Google pays them close attention. Because of this, webmasters use this service as much as ordinary backlinking.

For social bookmarking, the software to use is **Bookmarking Demon** and **Social Monkey**. For the big link building, use **Link Monster** and/or **SEnukeXCr**. These are the kinds of products that people offering five figure social bookmarking and link building gigs are using, including all of our group. Social monkey in particular is very easy to use. Link Monster is expensive, and that every month, but we make like 20 times that in return. SenukeXCr is a killer software that pretty much everybody uses. All instructions for how to use it come with it.

The main reason I don't list any advanced gigs that don't require software and extensive knowledge is the simple fact that complicated gigs would require too much work and time. Never forget that a gig pays only $4 on the front-end, with the potential to get a tip and the possibility to make some extra money if your customer orders an addition to your gig.

Not every creative idea is suitable for a Fiverr gig. In general, you shouldn't take longer than 15 minutes to complete an order for any gig; otherwise the gig takes too much of your time and costs money, if that time could be used on a different, less time-consuming gig. You might have good ideas for gigs, but if they are so complicated that you'd have to put them into an imaginary "Advanced Gigs" section of this book, then it's better to either forget about it right away or to try and come up with a lite version of the same gig. Software, however, automates everything. Hit a few buttons and you make hundreds of dollars, if you have many orders.

Creative Simple Gigs

In this section I want to list a whole number of gigs that are self-explanatory and don't need a step-by-step manual. It's mainly about creativity, ideas that you might not have thought of, but are able to use and recombine. Hopefully they can even serve as inspiration!

I will take a high-quality photo of anything you want in [your city]

I will take a high-quality photo of your logo stuck on my chest

I will take a high-quality photo of your logo written on my forehead

I will take a high-quality photo of my dog wearing your logo

I will send you a postcard from [your location, preferably exotic]

I will write your message in the sand on the beach and send you a photo

I will [do something funny] to reveal your message / text / web address

I will answer your question about [your profession]

I will draw a cute manga character / creature / chibi

I will draw one illustration for an article

I will design a cute character for you

I will colorize a small drawing of your choice

I will invite you to Google+

I will pin [number] pictures of your website on my pinterest account

I will create a QR code for your website (use Google QR generator)

I will be your boy-/girlfriend on Facebook (create a fake account)

I will honestly rate your attractiveness

I will listen to your problem and give you common sense advice

I will make a tough decision for you (be serious)

I will listen and respond to your confession

I will give you serious relationship advice

I will professionally edit your photo

I will write you a custom made love letter

I will write a 10 line poem on a subject of your choice

I will write a song for you

I will write a comment on your blog every day for five days / a week

I will answer 5 travel related questions about [place you know well]

I will answer 5 questions about [your country and people]

I will record a great video testimonial for you

I will write a short review of your product

I will do a professional 2 minute voice over for you

I will record myself playing a song of your choice on my [instrument]

I will record myself saying anything you want gangsta style

I will record myself singing a song of your choice

I will record myself singing a custom happy birthday song

I will record myself saying anything you want in a cartoon / celebrity voice

Reaching Beyond Fiverr

Like all pure blooded money forges, Fiverr has been cloned numerous times. It appears that the basic script used by Fiverr is also used by all these other websites, which even look and work very much the same way. However, unlike Fiverr, these websites generally allow you to choose different prices for your gigs.

Make no mistake, though. Fiverr is the ringleader and has much more traffic and potential then all of these other sites. Nonetheless, the material you have before you can be used just as well on the other sites, effectively increasing the likelihood to receive orders for the same services you're already offering on Fiverr.

The more gigs you have, the more individual orders you'll get, adding up to a hefty daily profit. It's all about the numbers! Even if your gigs only get one order every two days, if you have 20 gigs on Fiverr and the same amount of the other websites, you might very well have problems keeping up with all the orders. Here are the top 9 Fiverr clones at the time of writing this book.

GigBucks

TenBux

Zeerk

Dealerr

Uphype

JustaFive

GigMe5

GigsWood

GigHour

What's more, you can join the European versions of Fiverr, like the French or German version, and get 4€ instead of $4. Since the Euro is more valuable, you make more money for the same work. The only barrier might be the language, and there's also less traffic on these sites. Still, I got a few orders on the German Fiverr and made some money there.

What You Need to Avoid

Apart from the many ways you can make money on Fiverr, we also need to talk about things you need to avoid. A lot of people will only tell you what to do, but it's just as important to know what you shouldn't do, what doesn't work, and what'll simply get you into trouble. Now, I've already mentioned things you shouldn't do all throughout this book, but here are a few that really stand out and need their own section.

I want to begin with what's perhaps the biggest blunder of all.

Avoid 1 – The Scraper Method

I've seen software products that allow you to log into your Fiverr accounts, make new accounts, use proxies, check your messages, create new gigs and so on. The main promise behind such a product is its ability to go to a competitor's gig, scrape all the names of all the people who previously bought from this gig and then send a mass mail to each and every one of the usernames collected by the software. Such programs are advertised mainly for this ability, and it seems powerful at first, but all it'll do is get you into trouble. Whatever you do, don't fall for such a product and don't ever send unsolicited messages on Fiverr or any of the Fiverr clones!

When you send an unsolicited message on Fiverr, this is what it looks like to the recipient.

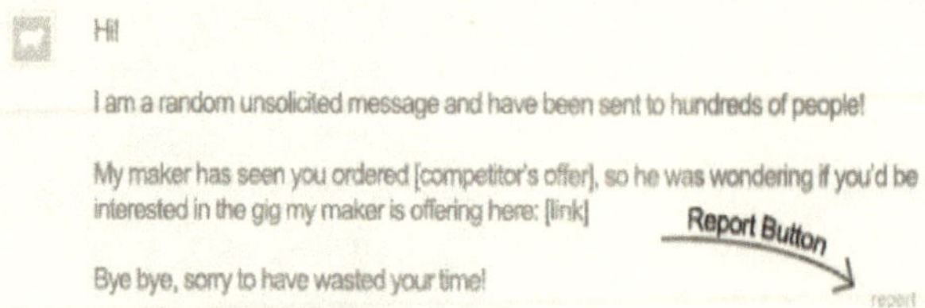

Imagine you're going about your business when your e-mail program suddenly alerts you of a new message on Fiverr. Of course, you think it's important – it must be a customer or an inquiry by a *potential* customer. So you stop what you're doing, go to Fiverr, login, look at the message and this is what you see. I'm 99% sure you'll click on the report button.

I always click on it. Remember that the experience assembled in this course is that of a group of 6-figure power sellers. Very early in our Fiverr career, two of us made the mistake to try the scraper method, despite my warnings.

The good thing about this is that we found out what actually happens when someone clicks the report button in response to unsolicited messages like this.

What happens is that the person who sent the message gets automatically banned from sending and receiving messages, which completely cripples your whole business. I had my friends talk to the customer support, apologize for their mistake and ask for their message capability to be restored. Gorgeous as the Fiverr support staff is, they quickly responded and accepted the apology. However, since there were so many messages involved, many other people clicked on that report button in the course of two or three days. Because of this, my friends were banned at least half a dozen times and had to grovel back to the support to explain that it was the aftermath of the mass mailing for which they had already apologized.

I'm sure I don't have to explain to you that you shouldn't do this. To top it all off, my friends didn't even get one extra customer from this action, because people simply won't respond positively to unsolicited messages.

Avoid 2 – The Bird Catcher

A few months ago I came across a report that explains a single idea for a gig, which is actually cumbersome on many levels. Funny what some people sell as guidebooks.

The Bird Catcher gig is the type of gig that promises to get you so-and-so many thousands of followers on Twitter, which is a service we've used ourselves in the Web Whisperer gig. However, actually getting this done is a pain and you're cheating your customers, which is something that doesn't agree with me at all.

First of all, let's talk about what you *can* do, then what you should avoid.

There's a website which used to be a "secret" back when only comparatively few people knew about it. Clever Internet marketers sold the information of its existence to other marketers and to people on Fiverr. This website is called **twiends.com** and it enables you to get Facebook likes and Twitter followers simply by liking other people's pages or following other people on Twitter. Each of these actions gives you a number of credits, which you can in turn use to buy your own followers and likes. Since the Facebook section has been removed, you can now only get Twitter followers from this website.

Obviously, you can do what other people have done ever since. Simply create a gig called:

"I will tell you how to get unlimited Twitter followers and Facebook likes for $5". It used to be a very good selling gig, because people want to know this, it was true and even worked. Indeed, you can still use it today. This is an example for the teacher gig, which I've outlined in the Gig Treasure Chest in section 2. There are other pages like twiends.com, such as **youlikehits.com** and they offer a lot more possibilities. So use them for such a gig if you want to. I believe they are still fairly "secret" today.

However, promising to give someone Twitter followers doesn't work like that. People who do this first register 100,000 Twitter accounts by automated means. Whenever they get an order on Fiverr, they simply follow that person with, let's say, 10,000 accounts in order to deliver what they promised. If they also offer an addition to their gig, promising 50,000 followers for $20, they do the same thing with a bunch of the other accounts they still have. What I want you to understand are two things. First, never order one of these gigs if you want to have followers that are responsive. Secondly, don't waste your time to find out how to offer such a gig yourself. If you actually had the (expensive) software and the proxies to pull this off, then I suppose you could do it. But like I said, it's a waste of time to find out how to do it and set it up, and you could easily do other gigs that pay more and don't require you to cheat your customer.

As a general advice, I want to stress again that if you wish to be a successful Internet marketer, you need learn early on to be the real deal and do things right. While I do give you a few options throughout this course that can be misused, you shouldn't do so. Personally, I want to be the real deal and deliver products and services that are actually worth it. People only want to follow and buy from someone who's trustworthy and intends to deliver, not one of those scammers or false gurus who simply want to get the money. So don't be one of these no-good people and you'll have learned something very important already!

Avoid 3 – Multiple Accounts

Since Fiverr only lets you have and run 20 gigs at the same time, and it's beneficial to have multiple versions of one type of gig, you will quickly run out of slots. The only solution for this problem is to create more than one account. As I stated in the introduction, this is not allowed by Fiverr itself and you need to be careful and decide for yourself whether or not you want to do it and gamble with your account.

However, since this isn't something were you cheat another person, but merely want to get more slots for your gigs, I have no problem with it. I never actually did it, though.

There are two things you need to remember when creating and managing multiple accounts. First, you need to use a proxy server to cloak your IP address whenever you log into one of your accounts. If you log into one account and then log into another account without changing your IP address, you might get into trouble. Obviously, a different family member could have a second account and use the same computer, but if you have three, four or five accounts, it's safe to say you'll definitely get in trouble.

Secondly, every Fiverr account needs to be connected to a PayPal account via an email address. In order to get around this problem, all you need to do is to log into your PayPal account and define more email addresses. You can define as many email addresses to link into your PayPal account as you want, which allows you to use these different addresses for your other Fiverr accounts. Be aware of it, though, that Fiverr is able to see your real name whenever you take money out of your Fiverr account. It has never happened to anyone I know, but in principle they could see that the people behind these different Fiverr accounts and email addresses are actually always the same person. Should that ever happen, it's likely all of those accounts get banned.

Avoid 4 – The Fast Banker

I understand that if you're new and make your first money online with Fiverr, you will be ecstatic and can't wait to get the money into your PayPal account to actually have it in your hand – or virtual hand for that matter. However, don't forget that PayPal charges a $1 fee for every transaction, which is why you should wait until you have accumulated a larger sum before you take it. This way, you minimize the PayPal fees!

Seven Ways to Promote your Gigs

In the introduction I explained how you need to construct your gigs in order to get people to buy from you rather than someone else. There are a number of means by which you can promote your gigs and get more people to see them, thereby increasing your chance to get customers. Always remember: the one thing you need to make sales on the Internet is traffic, so let's talk about a few ways to get it to your gigs.

1 – Be your own Ping Pong Man

In Easy Gig 9, I talked about the act of pinging, and how pinging a website brings it to the attention of the search engine providers. It's fairly obvious that you should be your own Ping Pong Man and ping your gigs, whenever you create or update them. In fact, you should ping them periodically, since every new feedback on your gig represents an update to the page.

The websites we used for our Ping Pong Man gig were:

www.pingfarm.com

www.feedshark.brainbliss.com

www.pingler.com

You can submit the URL of your gig on the sites for free and hopefully gain more attention this way.

2 – Create a Blog and Pages for your Gigs

Having a page dedicated for your gigs is very good idea in general, especially if you have a whole account that revolves around a certain topic. There are many ways in which you can create a website. I recommend you get your own domain name and webhosting, because it's superior to free solutions. You can get a domain name at **godaddy.com**, which is the best place to get domains, and webhosting on **hostgator.com**, one leading hosting providers and what I use myself. I recommend the baby hosting plan, since it's inexpensive and you can put as many websites on it as you want.

Now, you can log into your hostgator c-panel, start "Fantastico" and install A WordPress blog, which is all automated and takes only a few clicks. For more details, there are many tutorials on YouTube you can watch about how to customize your WordPress blog. If you have your own .com domain, you can actually rank in Google with it and potentially get a lot of people to your gig.

You can create a page on your blog for every gig you offer, where you write about it, offer more pictures and videos than the Fiverr gig description page allows you to put there. In addition, you can add some of the best reviews you get on your gig. One way to do this is to take a screenshot of your gig on Fiverr, cut out the comments section and put it on the site.

You can also go to blogger and open up a free blog, but it won't be quite as professional or much of a learning experience for you. If you have your own hosting, domain and WordPress blog installed, you can freely modify it and grow from the experience. Sooner or later in your Internet marketing career, you will *have* to get your own website, so you might as well make one for your gigs right away. With the money you earn on Fiverr, paying the small hosting fee should be no problem at all.

Remember to ping your website or the pages on it whenever you create or update them.

3 – Leverage Social Networks, Bookmarks and Facebook

Social networks are powerful platforms to share information with a large number of people, and have them share that information with even more people. Whenever you create a new gig on Fiverr, you should post on Facebook and write a tweet on your Twitter account, or perhaps even with more than one account to maximize your results.

When you're on Facebook, you should search for groups by using the keyword "Fiverr". You will come across groups such as the **official Fiverr group** and **Post Your Gigs**, which are great for promotion. So whenever you create a new gig, you should post on these groups.

Lastly, you can add your gig to social bookmarking sites, but if you don't have automated tools to do it, doing it by hand can be rather tedious. But since you are on Fiverr, you can simply order a social bookmarking service from another seller, using the funds you already have on your Fiverr account. Adding your gigs to a few social bookmarking sites by hand shouldn't be a problem or to tedious, so you can do that in the beginning.

4 – Forum Marketing

Forum marketing is all about getting people's attention by either mentioning a certain gig or having a link to your gig in your signature. If you go with the first option, you should make sure that you actually respond to someone's problem, and that your gig presents a solution to it. It might be beneficial if you appear to be separate from the gig you're mentioning and not the person actually offering it, as many people respond badly to advertisement and may not take your suggestion seriously, thinking you're just trying to sell them your service.

If you're promoting gigs related to Internet marketing, the best place to advertise them is in your signature on Warrior Forum, which is the main hub for Internet marketing on the planet and the known universe. The best way to do it is by using a banner, which costs a fee, but will get you a lot more attention. After a while, you can go back to using just a text link.

5 – Video Marketing

Another very simple method to bring people to your gig is to create videos, using **animoto** or **muvee Reveal**. In fact, you can use the exact same videos you are posting on your gig, so you already have them! Add your videos to YouTube and other video platforms to maximize your exposure. Put a link to your gig and website into the description of the video and you're set.

6 – Be Your Own Offliner

Yes indeed, offline marketing works if you live at the right location! In Medium Gig 5, we've talked about a gig where you design and post flyers in your city, so do that for yourself. Since you will be posting these flyers at the cafeteria of your local university, make sure your gig is useful to students. You could offer a teaching gig, where you tutor them in mathematics, programming or some other subject you are good at.

If you give your flyers to people in a crowded area, the same rule applies. Make sure your gig is useful to the people you might encounter. Personally, I'd go with the University option, because it's hard to give people a flyer directly. Putting it on cafeteria tables for everybody to see and pick up is much easier and more effective.

You might be wondering why you are even supposed to market Fiverr gigs and not just offer your private services, as that will get you around the Fiverr fee. The reason is that you'll get more sales and positive feedback, which in turn will boost both your seller level and authority in the eyes of potential customers who see your gig. It's about the pillar of growth!

7 – Classified Ads

There are hundreds of free online classified advertising venues, such as Craigslist, **epage.com** or **buckeyeads.com**. On all of these sites, you can post classified ads either for free or for a price to get a better position. This is a great way for you to reach a lot of eyes!

Final Words

Nothing happens on the Internet until something is sold. Fiverr is a colorful place and as such a place of many opportunities. Because of all this color, there is an endless amount of ways to use the services on Fiverr to make money, or simply sell your own services, if not both at the same time.

I've gone through great lengths to deliver a course of high quality to you, containing as much information and guidance as I thought was appropriate. My main ambition was not only to teach you about best-selling Gigs and how to complete them yourself, but to show you such a large number of possibilities that you might develop a certain level of creativity in these matters, so that you may find it easy to come up with your own ideas in the future.

As I now conclude this book, I believe to have over delivered, considering the small price tag I put on this course. And I am pleased, because that is exactly what I want my standards to be.